History's Warriors

NINJA

GAIL TERP

Black Rabbit Books

Bolt is published by Black Rabbit Books
P.O. Box 3263, Mankato, Minnesota, 56002.
www.blackrabbitbooks.com
Copyright © 2020 Black Rabbit Books

Marysa Storm, editor; Grant Gould, designer;
Omay Ayres, photo researcher

All rights reserved. No part of this book may be
reproduced, stored in a retrieval system or transmitted in any form
or by any means, electronic, mechanical, photocopying, recording, or
otherwise, without written permission from the publisher.

Names: Terp, Gail, 1951- author.
Title: Ninja / by Gail Terp.
Description: Mankato, Minnesota : Black Rabbit Books, [2020] |
Series: Bolt. History's warriors | Audience: 4-6. | Audience: 9-12. |
Summary: "Step back in time, and discover the lives ninja led through
labeled graphics, fun facts, and age-appropriate text that separates fact
from fiction while keeping readers interested and engaged"– Provided by
publisher. | Includes bibliographical references and index.
Identifiers: LCCN 2018009107 (print) | LCCN 2018033448 (ebook) |
ISBN 9781680728576 (e-book) | ISBN 9781680728514 (library binding) |
ISBN 9781644660423 (paperback)
Subjects: LCSH: Ninja–Japan–History–Juvenile literature.
Classification: LCC UB271.J3 (ebook) | LCC UB271.J3 T47 2020 (print) |
DDC 355.5/48-dc23
LC record available at https://lccn.loc.gov/2018009107

Printed in the United States. 1/19

Image Credits

Alamy: AF archive, 28 (TMNT);
Christian Weber, 22 (bow and arrows);
John Lander, 28 (top); Oldtime, 17; clipartxtras.
com: doe, 22–23 (ninja); TomTom, 4–5; commons.
wikimedia.org: Tsukioka Yoshitoshi, 9; Getty: BLOOM
image, 21 (ninja); iStock: duncan1890, 12; isegagne, 3; oros.
fotech.cl/: Usuari, 26–27; oursogo.com: Camouflage Jun, 24;
paping.org: webbkyrkan, 14–15; shop.1-72depot.com: Zvezda,
Cover; Shutterstock: 3DMI, 22 (throwing blades); A-R-T, 25; Barks,
10–11 (large map); Chrislofotos, 20; Fotokvadrat, 18; Martial Red,
29; phoelixDE, 1 (throwing blades), 31; pohwee_see, 23; rudall30,
32; Touseefdesigner.com, 21 (ladder); Vudhikrai, 1 (swords);
wallpaperswide.com: Light Farm Studios, 6–7; westsea.com:
West Sea, 22–23 (staff); zenjo.co.nz: ZENJO MARTIAL ARTS
SUPPLY, 22 (caltrops)
Every effort has been made to contact copyright
holders for material reproduced in this book. Any
omissions will be rectified in subsequent
printings if notice is given to the
publisher.

CONTENTS

CHAPTER 1
Meet the Ninja...........4

CHAPTER 2
Ninja Life................13

CHAPTER 3
Ninja in Action..........19

CHAPTER 4
The End
of the Ninja Age........26

Other Resources..........30

CHAPTER 1

Meet the NINJA

It was a moonless night. Three ninja crouched in the woods near a **fortress**. Their dark clothes kept them hidden. Nearby, their **warlord's** army waited. One ninja gave a quick signal. Silently, the three moved toward the moat. They swam swiftly across.

Sneaking In

One ninja threw a hook to the top of the building's wall. They all climbed up the attached rope. Still moving silently, they crept past the guards. The ninja then set a fire. They quickly escaped over the wall. As the fire distracted the guards, the army attacked.

Secretive Warriors

Ninja were warriors who lived in Japan. They were most active between the 1400s and 1600s. At that time, warlords controlled most of the land. Warlords fought each other constantly. They hired ninja for secretive tasks. Ninja acted as **assassins** and spies.

THE NINJA WORLD

Ninja came from what is now Japan's Mie and Shiga areas.

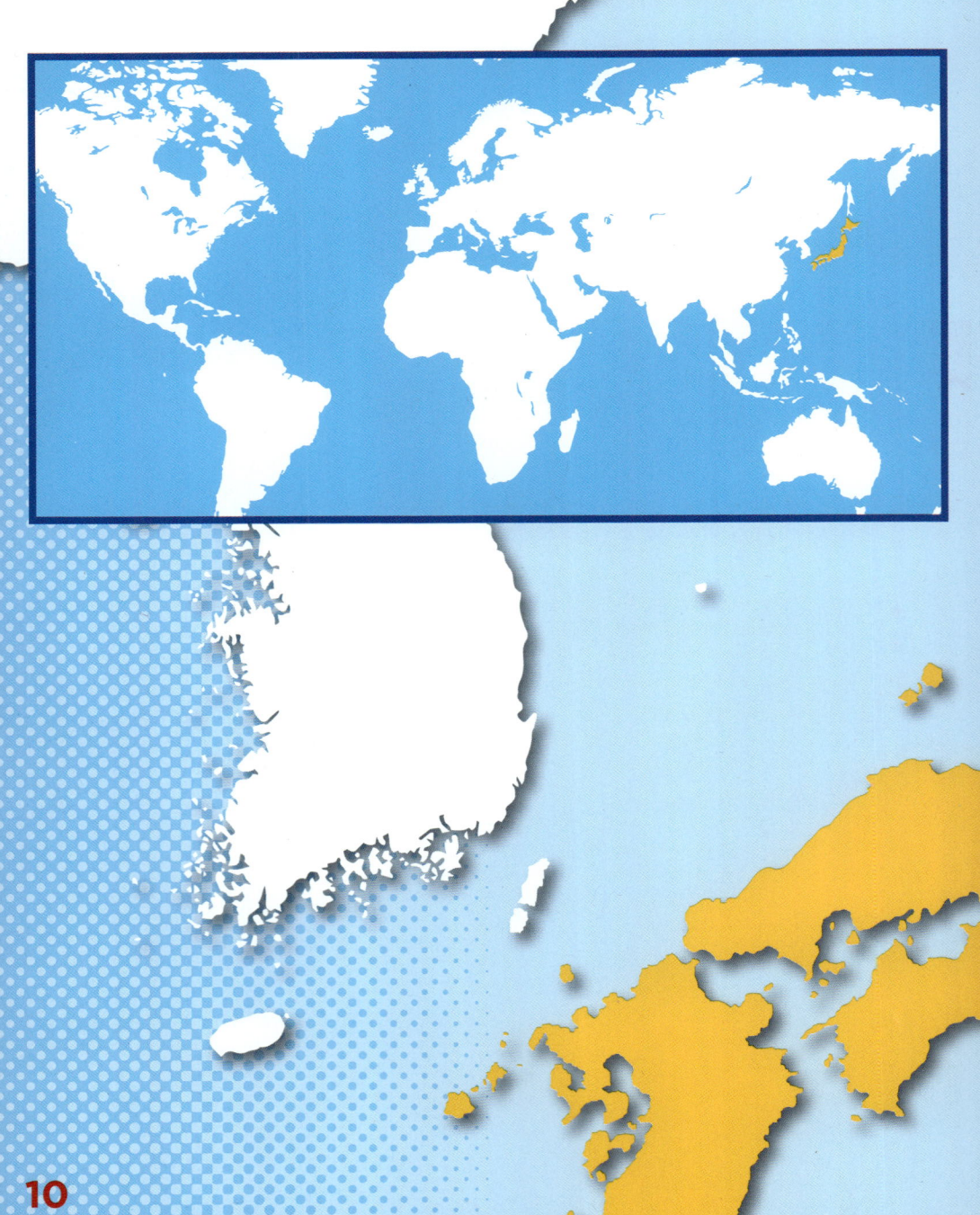

Ninja families joined together to form groups. Each group had three classes.

JONIN	CHUNIN	GENIN
heads of families	next in charge	ninja warriors
made big decisions	gave jobs to the genin	

CHAPTER 2

Ninja LIFE

Being a ninja was a family affair. Families often lived in mountains. Fathers taught their sons how to spy and fight. Only a few women were trained for the job.

NINJA HOUSE

Ninja lived in houses with many secret features. These features helped them in case of an attack.

HIDDEN STAIRCASES

TRAPS

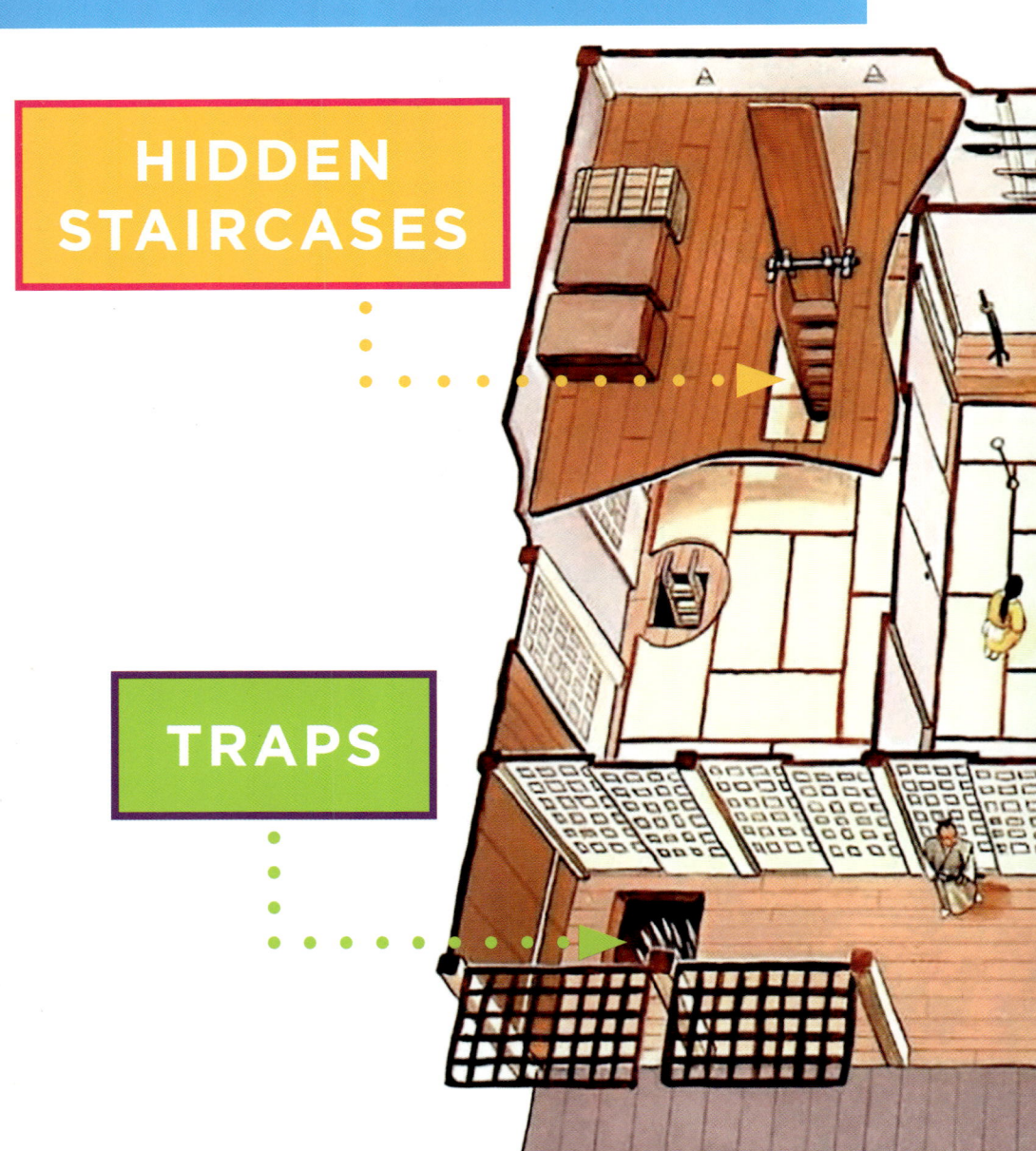

SECRET PASSAGES

HIDDEN EXITS

Ninja Training

Some families sent their children to ninja schools. Students trained constantly. They learned to run and walk silently. They practiced climbing walls and cliffs. Students mastered many different weapons too. They worked with swords, bows and arrows, and spears. They also practiced hand-to-hand **combat**.

Students didn't just train their bodies. They trained their minds too. They learned to solve problems and survive with few supplies.

To go unnoticed, ninja didn't eat food that caused bad breath.

Ninja had many disguises. They often dressed as performers. They also pretended to be farmers or **merchants**. On nighttime missions, they wore dark clothing.

CHAPTER 3

Ninja in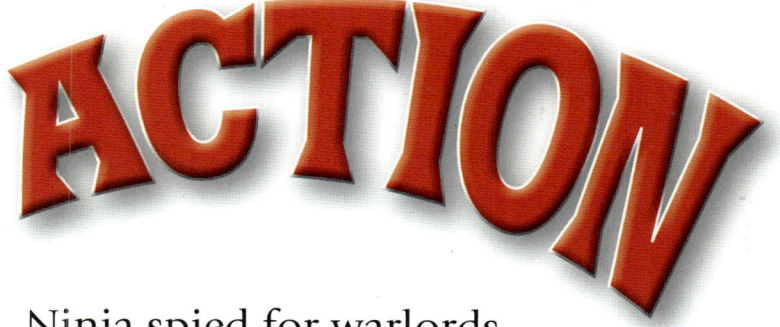

Ninja spied for warlords. They gathered information about their enemies. To get close, they'd often use disguises. Once they were in position, they'd watch and listen. Later, they'd have a lot to report.

As spies, ninja didn't want to be seen. They'd crouch down and appear to be rocks. They'd blend into shadows. Ninja moved without making a sound.

Entering an Enemy Fortress

Ninja often broke into enemy fortresses. Breaking in often started with crossing the moat. Ninja usually swam. They also floated on animal skins filled with air. Sometimes they used rafts.

Ninja then climbed the building's walls. They used rope ladders. Or they climbed with their hands and feet. Sometimes they slipped iron claws onto their hands for extra **grip**.

Climbing Walls

hands and feet

ladders

grappling hooks

WEAPONS AND CLOTHING

BOW AND ARROWS

THROWING BLADES

SWORD

Escape!

Once ninja finished a job, it was time to escape. If enemies noticed them, ninja sometimes threw smoke bombs. They also set off **explosives**. Or they tossed caltrops behind them. Enemies would step on these sharp tools. The caltrops would stop them in their tracks.

Ninja sometimes threw frogs or snakes at enemies to distract them.

CHAPTER 4

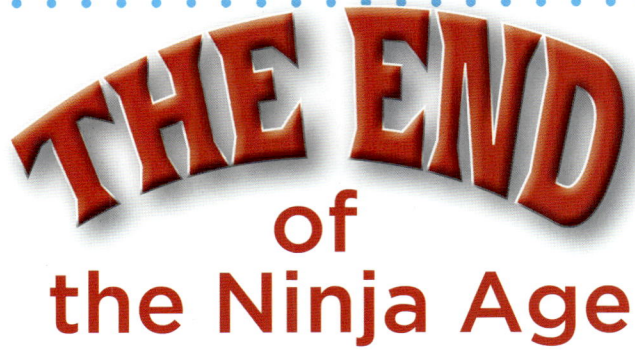

THE END of the Ninja Age

The age of the ninja couldn't last forever. In 1581, a powerful enemy warlord attacked a large group of ninja. After this battle, few members remained.

Then, in the 1600s, Japan had a long period of peace. Ninja were no longer needed for missions.

Ninja Influence

Ninja are no longer active. But people still like to learn about them. People can even go to ninja schools today.

Ninja life shows up in other places too. There are many ninja movies and TV shows. These warriors no longer exist. But their stories still influence the world today.

Ninja are often seen in pop culture. In 1983, two artists created the Teenage Mutant Ninja Turtles. People still enjoy movies about these characters today.

GLOSSARY

assassin (uh-SAS-in)—someone who kills another person usually for pay or from loyalty to a cause

combat (kahm-BAT)—active fighting, often in a war

explosive (ik-SPLOH-siv)—a device able to cause an explosion

feature (FEE-chur)—an interesting or important part or quality

fortress (FAWR-tris)—a place that is protected against attack

grappling hook (GRAP-ling HOOK)—a hook usually with multiple prongs that is typically attached to a rope and is used for grabbing or gripping

grip (GRIP)—the ability to hold firmly

merchant (MUR-chuhnt)—someone who buys and sells goods especially in large amounts

mutant (MYOOT-nt)—resulting from genetic mutation

warlord (WAWR-lawrd)—a leader of a military group that is not officially recognized

LEARN MORE

BOOKS

Dawson, Patricia. *Ninjas: Masters of Stealth and Secrecy.* History's Greatest Warriors. New York: Cavendish Square, 2015.

Hyde, Natalie. *Ninjas.* Crabtree Chrome. St. Catharines, Ontario: Crabtree Publishing, 2015.

Matthews, Rupert. *Ninjas.* History's Fearless Fighters. New York: Gareth Stevens Publishing, 2016.

WEBSITES

Can You Tell Which Ninja Fact is Real and Which is a Decoy?
www.cbc.ca/kidscbc2/the-feed/can-you-tell-which-ninja-fact-is-real-and-which-is-a-decoy

Japan
kids.nationalgeographic.com/explore/countries/japan/#japan-gardens.jpg

Ninja – History – Explore Japan
web-japan.org/kidsweb/explore/history/q4.html

INDEX

C
class systems, 12

D
disguises, 18, 19

F
families, 12, 13, 16

H
homes, 14–15

J
Japan, 8, 10–11

T
tools, 7, 20–21, 25

training, 13, 16

W
weapons, 16, 22–23